This notebook belongs to:

_____

Published by: Character Designs

UX Problem Statement Worksheet

Project name _____   Date:_____

User role: [   ]

	Activity	Reason
☐		
☐		
☐		

	Step	Obstacle	Negative Feeling
☐			
☐			
☐			

A _____ who feels _____

  USER ROLE   NEGATIVE FEELING

about _____ needs to _____

  REASON   STEP

but faces _____

  OBSTACLE

UX Problem Statement Worksheet

Project name _____   Date:_____

User role: [_____]

	Activity		Reason
☐			
☐			
☐			

	Step	Obstacle	Negative Feeling
☐			
☐			
☐			

A _____   who feels _____
      USER ROLE   NEGATIVE FEELING

about _____   needs to _____
         REASON   STEP

but faces _____
              OBSTACLE

UX Problem Statement Worksheet

Project name _____   Date:_____

User role: [   ]

	Activity	Reason
☐		
☐		
☐		

	Step	Obstacle	Negative Feeling
☐			
☐			
☐			

A _____ who feels _____
       USER ROLE   NEGATIVE FEELING

about _____ needs to _____
       REASON   STEP

but faces _____
               OBSTACLE

UX Problem Statement Worksheet

Project name _____   Date:_____

User role: [   ]

	Activity	Reason
☐		
☐		
☐		

	Step	Obstacle	Negative Feeling
☐			
☐			
☐			

A _____ who feels _____
       USER ROLE   NEGATIVE FEELING

about _____ needs to _____
       REASON   STEP

but faces _____
       OBSTACLE

UX Problem Statement Worksheet

Project name _____   Date: _____

User role: [   ]

	Activity	Reason
☐		
☐		
☐		

	Step	Obstacle	Negative Feeling
☐			
☐			
☐			

A _____ who feels _____
        USER ROLE   NEGATIVE FEELING

about _____ needs to _____
        REASON   STEP

but faces _____
            OBSTACLE

UX Problem Statement Worksheet

Project name _____   Date: _____

User role: [   ]

	Activity	Reason
☐		
☐		
☐		

	Step	Obstacle	Negative Feeling
☐			
☐			
☐			

A _____   who feels _____
         USER ROLE   NEGATIVE FEELING

about _____   needs to _____
         REASON   STEP

but faces _____
                   OBSTACLE

UX Problem Statement Worksheet

Project name _____   Date: _____

User role: [   ]

	Activity	Reason
☐		
☐		
☐		

	Step	Obstacle	Negative Feeling
☐			
☐			
☐			

A _____ who feels _____
        USER ROLE   NEGATIVE FEELING

about _____ needs to _____
          REASON   STEP

but faces _____
                OBSTACLE

UX Problem Statement Worksheet

Project name _____   Date:_____

User role: [   ]

	Activity	Reason
☐		
☐		
☐		

	Step	Obstacle	Negative Feeling
☐			
☐			
☐			

A _____ who feels _____
  USER ROLE   NEGATIVE FEELING

about _____ needs to _____
       REASON   STEP

but faces _____
              OBSTACLE

UX Problem Statement Worksheet

Project name _____   Date: _____

User role: [   ]

	Activity	Reason
☐		
☐		
☐		

	Step	Obstacle	Negative Feeling
☐			
☐			
☐			

A _____ who feels _____
         USER ROLE   NEGATIVE FEELING

about _____ needs to _____
              REASON   STEP

but faces _____
                    OBSTACLE

UX Problem Statement Worksheet

Project name _____   Date: _____

User role: [   ]

	Activity	Reason
☐		
☐		
☐		

	Step	Obstacle	Negative Feeling
☐			
☐			
☐			

A _____ who feels _____
    USER ROLE   NEGATIVE FEELING

about _____ needs to _____
    REASON   STEP

but faces _____
    OBSTACLE

UX Problem Statement Worksheet

User role: [   ]

	Activity	Reason
☐		
☐		
☐		

	Step	Obstacle	Negative Feeling
☐			
☐			
☐			

A _____ who feels _____
  USER ROLE   NEGATIVE FEELING

about _____ needs to _____
  REASON   STEP

but faces _____
  OBSTACLE

UX Problem Statement Worksheet

Project name _____   Date:_____

User role: [   ]

	Activity	Reason
☐		
☐		
☐		

	Step	Obstacle	Negative Feeling
☐			
☐			
☐			

A _____ who feels _____
      USER ROLE   NEGATIVE FEELING

about _____ needs to _____
      REASON   STEP

but faces _____
      OBSTACLE

UX Problem Statement Worksheet

Project name _____   Date: _____

User role: [   ]

	Activity	Reason
☐		
☐		
☐		

	Step	Obstacle	Negative Feeling
☐			
☐			
☐			

A _____ who feels _____

USER ROLE   NEGATIVE FEELING

about _____ needs to _____

REASON   STEP

but faces _____

OBSTACLE

UX Problem Statement Worksheet

Project name _____   Date: _____

User role: [_____]

	Activity	Reason
☐		
☐		
☐		

	Step	Obstacle	Negative Feeling
☐			
☐			
☐			

A _____ who feels _____

USER ROLE   NEGATIVE FEELING

about _____ needs to _____

REASON   STEP

but faces _____

OBSTACLE

UX Problem Statement Worksheet

Project name _____   Date: _____

User role: [   ]

	Activity	Reason
☐		
☐		
☐		

	Step	Obstacle	Negative Feeling
☐			
☐			
☐			

A _____ who feels _____

         USER ROLE   NEGATIVE FEELING

about _____ needs to _____

         REASON   STEP

but faces _____

                     OBSTACLE

UX Problem Statement Worksheet

Project name _____   Date: _____

User role: [_____]

	Activity	Reason
☐		
☐		
☐		

	Step	Obstacle	Negative Feeling
☐			
☐			
☐			

A _____ who feels _____

about _____ needs to _____

but faces _____

UX Problem Statement Worksheet

Project name _____   Date: _____

User role: [   ]

	Activity	Reason
☐		
☐		
☐		

	Step	Obstacle	Negative Feeling
☐			
☐			
☐			

A _____   who feels _____
    USER ROLE   NEGATIVE FEELING

about _____   needs to _____
    REASON   STEP

but faces _____
    OBSTACLE

UX Problem Statement Worksheet

Project name _____   Date: _____

User role: [_____]

	Activity	Reason
☐		
☐		
☐		

	Step	Obstacle	Negative Feeling
☐			
☐			
☐			

A _____ who feels _____
        USER ROLE   NEGATIVE FEELING

about _____ needs to _____
       REASON   STEP

but faces _____
               OBSTACLE

UX Problem Statement Worksheet

Project name _____   Date: _____

User role: [_____]

	Activity	Reason
☐		
☐		
☐		

	Step	Obstacle	Negative Feeling
☐			
☐			
☐			

A _____ who feels _____

    USER ROLE   NEGATIVE FEELING

about _____ needs to _____

    REASON   STEP

but faces _____

                  OBSTACLE

UX Problem Statement Worksheet

Project name _____   Date: _____

User role: [   ]

	Activity	Reason
☐		
☐		
☐		

	Step	Obstacle	Negative Feeling
☐			
☐			
☐			

A _____ who feels _____

     USER ROLE   NEGATIVE FEELING

about _____ needs to _____

     REASON   STEP

but faces _____

                     OBSTACLE

UX Problem Statement Worksheet

Project name _____   Date: _____

User role: [   ]

	Activity	Reason
☐		
☐		
☐		

	Step	Obstacle	Negative Feeling
☐			
☐			
☐			

A _____ who feels _____

USER ROLE   NEGATIVE FEELING

about _____ needs to _____

REASON   STEP

but faces _____

OBSTACLE

UX Problem Statement Worksheet

Project name _____   Date: _____

User role: [_____]

	Activity	Reason
☐		
☐		
☐		

	Step	Obstacle	Negative Feeling
☐			
☐			
☐			

A _____ who feels _____
       USER ROLE   NEGATIVE FEELING

about _____ needs to _____
       REASON   STEP

but faces _____
            OBSTACLE

UX Problem Statement Worksheet

User role: [   ]

Activity	Reason
☐	
☐	
☐	

Step	Obstacle	Negative Feeling
☐		
☐		
☐		

A _____ who feels _____

USER ROLE   NEGATIVE FEELING

about _____ needs to _____

REASON   STEP

but faces _____

OBSTACLE

UX Problem Statement Worksheet

Project name _____   Date:_____

User role: [   ]

	Activity	Reason
☐		
☐		
☐		

	Step	Obstacle	Negative Feeling
☐			
☐			
☐			

A _____ who feels _____

  USER ROLE   NEGATIVE FEELING

about _____ needs to _____

  REASON   STEP

but faces _____

  OBSTACLE

UX Problem Statement Worksheet

Project name _____   Date: _____

User role: [   ]

	Activity	Reason
☐		
☐		
☐		

	Step	Obstacle	Negative Feeling
☐			
☐			
☐			

A _____ who feels _____
       USER ROLE   NEGATIVE FEELING

about _____ needs to _____
       REASON   STEP

but faces _____
       OBSTACLE

UX Problem Statement Worksheet

Project name _____   Date:_____

User role: [   ]

	Activity	Reason
☐		
☐		
☐		

	Step	Obstacle	Negative Feeling
☐			
☐			
☐			

A _____ who feels _____
    USER ROLE   NEGATIVE FEELING

about _____ needs to _____
        REASON   STEP

but faces _____
              OBSTACLE

UX Problem Statement Worksheet

Project name _____   Date: _____

User role: [   ]

	Activity	Reason
☐		
☐		
☐		

	Step	Obstacle	Negative Feeling
☐			
☐			
☐			

A _____ who feels _____
   USER ROLE   NEGATIVE FEELING

about _____ needs to _____
      REASON   STEP

but faces _____
          OBSTACLE

UX Problem Statement Worksheet

Project name _____

User role: [   ]

	Activity	Reason
☐		
☐		
☐		

	Step	Obstacle	Negative Feeling
☐			
☐			
☐			

A _____ who feels _____
       USER ROLE   NEGATIVE FEELING

about _____ needs to _____
          REASON   STEP

but faces _____
                OBSTACLE

UX Problem Statement Worksheet

Project name _____   Date: _____

User role: [   ]

	Activity	Reason
☐		
☐		
☐		

	Step	Obstacle	Negative Feeling
☐			
☐			
☐			

A _____ who feels _____

    USER ROLE   NEGATIVE FEELING

about _____ needs to _____

    REASON   STEP

but faces _____

            OBSTACLE

UX Problem Statement Worksheet

Project name _____   Date: _____

User role: [   ]

	Activity	Reason
☐		
☐		
☐		

	Step	Obstacle	Negative Feeling
☐			
☐			
☐			

A _____ who feels _____
     USER ROLE   NEGATIVE FEELING

about _____ needs to _____
          REASON   STEP

but faces _____
               OBSTACLE

UX Problem Statement Worksheet

Project name _____   Date: _____

User role: [   ]

	Activity	Reason
☐		
☐		
☐		

	Step	Obstacle	Negative Feeling
☐			
☐			
☐			

A _____ who feels _____

       USER ROLE   NEGATIVE FEELING

about _____ needs to _____

       REASON   STEP

but faces _____

                   OBSTACLE

UX Problem Statement Worksheet

Project name _____   Date:_____

User role: [   ]

	Activity	Reason
☐		
☐		
☐		

	Step	Obstacle	Negative Feeling
☐			
☐			
☐			

A _____   who feels _____
    USER ROLE   NEGATIVE FEELING

about _____   needs to _____
       REASON   STEP

but faces _____
          OBSTACLE

UX Problem Statement Worksheet

Project name _____   Date: _____

User role: [   ]

	Activity	Reason
☐		
☐		
☐		

	Step	Obstacle	Negative Feeling
☐			
☐			
☐			

A _____ who feels _____
                    USER ROLE   NEGATIVE FEELING

about _____ needs to _____
                    REASON   STEP

but faces _____
                    OBSTACLE

UX Problem Statement Worksheet

Project name _____   Date:_____

User role: [_____]

	Activity	Reason
☐		
☐		
☐		

	Step	Obstacle	Negative Feeling
☐			
☐			
☐			

A _____ who feels _____
      USER ROLE   NEGATIVE FEELING

about _____ needs to _____
           REASON   STEP

but faces _____
              OBSTACLE

UX Problem Statement Worksheet

Project name _____   Date: _____

User role: [   ]

	Activity	Reason
☐		
☐		
☐		

	Step	Obstacle	Negative Feeling
☐			
☐			
☐			

A _____ who feels _____
        USER ROLE   NEGATIVE FEELING

about _____ needs to _____
         REASON   STEP

but faces _____
              OBSTACLE

UX Problem Statement Worksheet

Project name _____   Date: _____

User role: [_____]

	Activity	Reason
☐		
☐		
☐		

	Step	Obstacle	Negative Feeling
☐			
☐			
☐			

A _____ who feels _____

　　　USER ROLE　　　　　　　　　　　NEGATIVE FEELING

about _____ needs to _____

　　　REASON　　　　　　　　　　　　STEP

but faces _____

　　　　　　　OBSTACLE

UX Problem Statement Worksheet

Project name _____   Date: _____

User role: [   ]

	Activity	Reason
☐		
☐		
☐		

	Step	Obstacle	Negative Feeling
☐			
☐			
☐			

A _____ who feels _____

USER ROLE   NEGATIVE FEELING

about _____ needs to _____

REASON   STEP

but faces _____

OBSTACLE

UX Problem Statement Worksheet

Project name _____   Date: _____

User role: [   ]

	Activity	Reason
☐		
☐		
☐		

	Step	Obstacle	Negative Feeling
☐			
☐			
☐			

A _____ who feels _____
    USER ROLE   NEGATIVE FEELING

about _____ needs to _____
        REASON   STEP

but faces _____
            OBSTACLE

UX Problem Statement Worksheet

Project name _____   Date: _____

User role: [_____]

	Activity	Reason
☐		
☐		
☐		

	Step	Obstacle	Negative Feeling
☐			
☐			
☐			

A _____ who feels _____
        USER ROLE   NEGATIVE FEELING

about _____ needs to _____
          REASON   STEP

but faces _____
              OBSTACLE

UX Problem Statement Worksheet

User role: [   ]

	Activity	Reason
☐		
☐		
☐		

	Step	Obstacle	Negative Feeling
☐			
☐			
☐			

A _____ who feels _____
     USER ROLE   NEGATIVE FEELING

about _____ needs to _____
          REASON   STEP

but faces _____
                    OBSTACLE

UX Problem Statement Worksheet

Project name _____   Date:_____

User role: [   ]

	Activity	Reason
☐		
☐		
☐		

	Step	Obstacle	Negative Feeling
☐			
☐			
☐			

A _____ who feels _____

      USER ROLE   NEGATIVE FEELING

about _____ needs to _____

      REASON   STEP

but faces _____

                              OBSTACLE

UX Problem Statement Worksheet

Project name _____   Date: _____

User role: [   ]

	Activity	Reason
☐		
☐		
☐		

	Step	Obstacle	Negative Feeling
☐			
☐			
☐			

A _____ who feels _____
       USER ROLE   NEGATIVE FEELING

about _____ needs to _____
       REASON   STEP

but faces _____
       OBSTACLE

UX Problem Statement Worksheet

Project name _____   Date: _____

User role: [   ]

	Activity	Reason
☐		
☐		
☐		

	Step	Obstacle	Negative Feeling
☐			
☐			
☐			

A _____ who feels _____
    USER ROLE   NEGATIVE FEELING

about _____ needs to _____
        REASON   STEP

but faces _____
              OBSTACLE

UX Problem Statement Worksheet

Project name _____   Date: _____

User role: [   ]

	Activity	Reason
☐		
☐		
☐		

	Step	Obstacle	Negative Feeling
☐			
☐			
☐			

A _____ who feels _____
    USER ROLE   NEGATIVE FEELING

about _____ needs to _____
      REASON   STEP

but faces _____
                    OBSTACLE

UX Problem Statement Worksheet

Project name _____   Date: _____

User role: [_____]

	Activity	Reason
☐		
☐		
☐		

	Step	Obstacle	Negative Feeling
☐			
☐			
☐			

A _____ who feels _____
       USER ROLE   NEGATIVE FEELING

about _____ needs to _____
       REASON   STEP

but faces _____
                        OBSTACLE

UX Problem Statement Worksheet

Project name _____   Date: _____

User role: _____

	Activity	Reason
☐		
☐		
☐		

	Step	Obstacle	Negative Feeling
☐			
☐			
☐			

A _____ who feels _____
  USER ROLE   NEGATIVE FEELING

about _____ needs to _____
  REASON   STEP

but faces _____
  OBSTACLE

UX Problem Statement Worksheet

Project name _____   Date: _____

User role: [   ]

	Activity	Reason
☐		
☐		
☐		

	Step	Obstacle	Negative Feeling
☐			
☐			
☐			

A _____ who feels _____
    USER ROLE   NEGATIVE FEELING

about _____ needs to _____
      REASON   STEP

but faces _____
          OBSTACLE

UX Problem Statement Worksheet

Project name _____   Date:_____

User role: [   ]

	Activity	Reason
☐		
☐		
☐		

	Step	Obstacle	Negative Feeling
☐			
☐			
☐			

A _____ who feels _____
       USER ROLE   NEGATIVE FEELING

about _____ needs to _____
       REASON   STEP

but faces _____
       OBSTACLE

UX Problem Statement Worksheet

Project name _____   Date: _____

User role: [   ]

	Activity	Reason
☐		
☐		
☐		

	Step	Obstacle	Negative Feeling
☐			
☐			
☐			

A _____ who feels _____

USER ROLE   NEGATIVE FEELING

about _____ needs to _____

REASON   STEP

but faces _____

OBSTACLE

UX Problem Statement Worksheet

Project name _____   Date:_____

User role: [   ]

	Activity	Reason
☐		
☐		
☐		

	Step	Obstacle	Negative Feeling
☐			
☐			
☐			

A _____ who feels _____
  USER ROLE   NEGATIVE FEELING

about _____ needs to _____
  REASON   STEP

but faces _____
  OBSTACLE

UX Problem Statement Worksheet

Project name _____   Date: _____

User role: [   ]

	Activity	Reason
☐		
☐		
☐		

	Step	Obstacle	Negative Feeling
☐			
☐			
☐			

A _____ who feels _____
       USER ROLE   NEGATIVE FEELING

about _____ needs to _____
      REASON   STEP

but faces _____
                  OBSTACLE

UX Problem Statement Worksheet

Project name _____   Date: _____

User role: [_____]

	Activity	Reason
☐		
☐		
☐		

	Step	Obstacle	Negative Feeling
☐			
☐			
☐			

A _____ who feels _____

       USER ROLE   NEGATIVE FEELING

about _____ needs to _____

       REASON   STEP

but faces _____

                    OBSTACLE

UX Problem Statement Worksheet

Project name _____   Date:_____

User role: [   ]

	Activity	Reason
☐		
☐		
☐		

	Step	Obstacle	Negative Feeling
☐			
☐			
☐			

A   who feels

    USER ROLE   NEGATIVE FEELING

about   needs to

    REASON   STEP

but faces

    OBSTACLE

UX Problem Statement Worksheet

Project name _____   Date:_____

User role: [   ]

	Activity	Reason
☐		
☐		
☐		

	Step	Obstacle	Negative Feeling
☐			
☐			
☐			

A _____ who feels _____
   USER ROLE   NEGATIVE FEELING

about _____ needs to _____
      REASON   STEP

but faces _____
          OBSTACLE

UX Problem Statement Worksheet

Project name _____   Date: _____

User role: [   ]

	Activity	Reason
☐		
☐		
☐		

	Step	Obstacle	Negative Feeling
☐			
☐			
☐			

A _____ who feels _____
   USER ROLE   NEGATIVE FEELING

about _____ needs to _____
   REASON   STEP

but faces _____
                        OBSTACLE

UX Problem Statement Worksheet

Project name _____   Date:_____

User role: [   ]

	Activity	Reason
☐		
☐		
☐		

	Step	Obstacle	Negative Feeling
☐			
☐			
☐			

A _____ who feels _____
      USER ROLE   NEGATIVE FEELING

about _____ needs to _____
      REASON   STEP

but faces _____
             OBSTACLE

UX Problem Statement Worksheet

Project name _____   Date:_____

User role: [   ]

	Activity	Reason
☐		
☐		
☐		

	Step	Obstacle	Negative Feeling
☐			
☐			
☐			

A _____ who feels _____
        USER ROLE   NEGATIVE FEELING

about _____ needs to _____
        REASON   STEP

but faces _____
        OBSTACLE

UX Problem Statement Worksheet

Project name _____ Date: _____

User role: [   ]

	Activity	Reason
☐		
☐		
☐		

	Step	Obstacle	Negative Feeling
☐			
☐			
☐			

A _____ who feels _____
     USER ROLE   NEGATIVE FEELING

about _____ needs to _____
     REASON   STEP

but faces _____
     OBSTACLE

UX Problem Statement Worksheet

Project name _____   Date: _____

User role: [   ]

	Activity	Reason
☐		
☐		
☐		

	Step	Obstacle	Negative Feeling
☐			
☐			
☐			

A _____ who feels _____
   USER ROLE   NEGATIVE FEELING

about _____ needs to _____
      REASON   STEP

but faces _____
                         OBSTACLE

UX Problem Statement Worksheet

Project name _____   Date: _____

User role: [   ]

	Activity	Reason
☐		
☐		
☐		

	Step	Obstacle	Negative Feeling
☐			
☐			
☐			

A _____ who feels _____

USER ROLE   NEGATIVE FEELING

about _____ needs to _____

REASON   STEP

but faces _____

OBSTACLE

UX Problem Statement Worksheet

Project name _____   Date: _____

User role: [   ]

	Activity	Reason
☐		
☐		
☐		

	Step	Obstacle	Negative Feeling
☐			
☐			
☐			

A _____ who feels _____
    USER ROLE   NEGATIVE FEELING

about _____ needs to _____
         REASON   STEP

but faces _____
             OBSTACLE

UX Problem Statement Worksheet

Project name _____   Date: _____

User role: [_____]

	Activity	Reason
☐		
☐		
☐		

	Step	Obstacle	Negative Feeling
☐			
☐			
☐			

A _____ who feels _____
     USER ROLE   NEGATIVE FEELING

about _____ needs to _____
     REASON   STEP

but faces _____
     OBSTACLE

UX Problem Statement Worksheet

Project name _____   Date: _____

User role: [   ]

	Activity	Reason
☐		
☐		
☐		

	Step	Obstacle	Negative Feeling
☐			
☐			
☐			

A _____ who feels _____
        USER ROLE   NEGATIVE FEELING

about _____ needs to _____
            REASON   STEP

but faces _____
                        OBSTACLE

UX Problem Statement Worksheet

Project name _____   Date: _____

User role:		

	Activity	Reason
☐		
☐		
☐		

	Step	Obstacle	Negative Feeling
☐			
☐			
☐			

A _____ who feels _____
  USER ROLE   NEGATIVE FEELING

about _____ needs to _____
        REASON   STEP

but faces _____
              OBSTACLE

UX Problem Statement Worksheet

Project name _____   Date: _____

User role: [   ]

	Activity	Reason
☐		
☐		
☐		

	Step	Obstacle	Negative Feeling
☐			
☐			
☐			

A _____ who feels _____
  USER ROLE   NEGATIVE FEELING

about _____ needs to _____
       REASON   STEP

but faces _____
           OBSTACLE

UX Problem Statement Worksheet

Project name _____   Date:_____

User role:	

	Activity	Reason
☐		
☐		
☐		

	Step	Obstacle	Negative Feeling
☐			
☐			
☐			

A _____ who feels _____

          USER ROLE   NEGATIVE FEELING

about _____ needs to _____

        REASON   STEP

but faces _____

        OBSTACLE

UX Problem Statement Worksheet

Project name _____   Date: _____

User role: [   ]

	Activity	Reason
☐		
☐		
☐		

	Step	Obstacle	Negative Feeling
☐			
☐			
☐			

A _____ who feels _____

    USER ROLE   NEGATIVE FEELING

about _____ needs to _____

    REASON   STEP

but faces _____

                            OBSTACLE

UX Problem Statement Worksheet

Project name _____   Date: _____

User role: [   ]

	Activity	Reason
☐		
☐		
☐		

	Step	Obstacle	Negative Feeling
☐			
☐			
☐			

A _____ who feels _____
      USER ROLE   NEGATIVE FEELING

about _____ needs to _____
      REASON   STEP

but faces _____
      OBSTACLE

UX Problem Statement Worksheet

Project name _____   Date: _____

User role: [   ]

	Activity	Reason
☐		
☐		
☐		

	Step	Obstacle	Negative Feeling
☐			
☐			
☐			

A _____ who feels _____

        USER ROLE   NEGATIVE FEELING

about _____ needs to _____

        REASON   STEP

but faces _____

        OBSTACLE

UX Problem Statement Worksheet

Project name _____   Date: _____

User role: [   ]

	Activity	Reason
☐		
☐		
☐		

	Step	Obstacle	Negative Feeling
☐			
☐			
☐			

A _____   who feels _____
   USER ROLE   NEGATIVE FEELING

about _____   needs to _____
      REASON   STEP

but faces _____
          OBSTACLE

UX Problem Statement Worksheet

Project name _____   Date:_____

User role: [   ]

	Activity	Reason
☐		
☐		
☐		

	Step	Obstacle	Negative Feeling
☐			
☐			
☐			

A _____ who feels _____
　　　　　USER ROLE　　　　　　　　　　　　　NEGATIVE FEELING

about _____ needs to _____
　　　　　REASON　　　　　　　　　　　　　STEP

but faces _____
　　　　　OBSTACLE

UX Problem Statement Worksheet

Project name _____   Date:_____

User role: [   ]

	Activity	Reason
☐		
☐		
☐		

	Step	Obstacle	Negative Feeling
☐			
☐			
☐			

A _____ who feels _____
      USER ROLE   NEGATIVE FEELING

about _____ needs to _____
          REASON   STEP

but faces _____
                    OBSTACLE

UX Problem Statement Worksheet

Project name _____   Date:_____

User role: [   ]

	Activity	Reason
☐		
☐		
☐		

	Step	Obstacle	Negative Feeling
☐			
☐			
☐			

A _____ who feels _____
        USER ROLE   NEGATIVE FEELING

about _____ needs to _____
          REASON   STEP

but faces _____
              OBSTACLE

UX Problem Statement Worksheet

Project name _____   Date: _____

User role: [   ]

	Activity	Reason
☐		
☐		
☐		

	Step	Obstacle	Negative Feeling
☐			
☐			
☐			

A _____ who feels _____

       USER ROLE   NEGATIVE FEELING

about _____ needs to _____

       REASON   STEP

but faces _____

       OBSTACLE

UX Problem Statement Worksheet

Project name _____   Date: _____

User role: [   ]

	Activity	Reason
☐		
☐		
☐		

	Step	Obstacle	Negative Feeling
☐			
☐			
☐			

A _____ who feels _____
       USER ROLE   NEGATIVE FEELING

about _____ needs to _____
       REASON   STEP

but faces _____
           OBSTACLE

UX Problem Statement Worksheet

Project name _____   Date: _____

User role: [_____]

	Activity	Reason
☐		
☐		
☐		

	Step	Obstacle	Negative Feeling
☐			
☐			
☐			

A _____ who feels _____
     USER ROLE   NEGATIVE FEELING

about _____ needs to _____
     REASON   STEP

but faces _____
                       OBSTACLE

UX Problem Statement Worksheet

Project name _____ Date: _____

User role:

	Activity	Reason
☐		
☐		
☐		

	Step	Obstacle	Negative Feeling
☐			
☐			
☐			

A _____ who feels _____

USER ROLE   NEGATIVE FEELING

about _____ needs to _____

REASON   STEP

but faces _____

OBSTACLE

UX Problem Statement Worksheet

Project name _____   Date: _____

User role: [   ]

	Activity	Reason
☐		
☐		
☐		

	Step	Obstacle	Negative Feeling
☐			
☐			
☐			

A _____ who feels _____

USER ROLE   NEGATIVE FEELING

about _____ needs to _____

REASON   STEP

but faces _____

OBSTACLE

UX Problem Statement Worksheet

Project name _____   Date:_____

User role: [   ]

	Activity	Reason
☐		
☐		
☐		

	Step	Obstacle	Negative Feeling
☐			
☐			
☐			

A _____ who feels _____
       USER ROLE   NEGATIVE FEELING

about _____ needs to _____
      REASON   STEP

but faces _____
                        OBSTACLE

UX Problem Statement Worksheet

Project name _____   Date: _____

User role: [   ]

	Activity	Reason
☐		
☐		
☐		

	Step	Obstacle	Negative Feeling
☐			
☐			
☐			

A _____ who feels _____
        USER ROLE   NEGATIVE FEELING

about _____ needs to _____
        REASON   STEP

but faces _____
                          OBSTACLE

UX Problem Statement Worksheet

Project name _____   Date:_____

User role: [   ]

	Activity	Reason
☐		
☐		
☐		

	Step	Obstacle	Negative Feeling
☐			
☐			
☐			

A _____ who feels _____
          USER ROLE   NEGATIVE FEELING

about _____ needs to _____
          REASON   STEP

but faces _____
                OBSTACLE

UX Problem Statement Worksheet

Project name _____   Date: _____

User role: [   ]

	Activity	Reason
☐		
☐		
☐		

	Step	Obstacle	Negative Feeling
☐			
☐			
☐			

A _____ who feels _____
         USER ROLE   NEGATIVE FEELING

about _____ needs to _____
         REASON   STEP

but faces _____
                    OBSTACLE

UX Problem Statement Worksheet

Project name _____   Date: _____

User role: [_____]

	Activity	Reason
☐		
☐		
☐		

	Step	Obstacle	Negative Feeling
☐			
☐			
☐			

A _____ who feels _____
        USER ROLE   NEGATIVE FEELING

about _____ needs to _____
            REASON   STEP

but faces _____
                OBSTACLE

UX Problem Statement Worksheet

Project name _____   Date: _____

User role: [   ]

	Activity	Reason
☐		
☐		
☐		

	Step	Obstacle	Negative Feeling
☐			
☐			
☐			

A _____ who feels _____
        USER ROLE   NEGATIVE FEELING

about _____ needs to _____
        REASON   STEP

but faces _____
        OBSTACLE

UX Problem Statement Worksheet

Project name _____   Date: _____

User role: [   ]

	Activity	Reason
☐		
☐		
☐		

	Step	Obstacle	Negative Feeling
☐			
☐			
☐			

A _____ who feels _____
       USER ROLE   NEGATIVE FEELING

about _____ needs to _____
           REASON   STEP

but faces _____
                      OBSTACLE

UX Problem Statement Worksheet

Project name _____   Date: _____

User role: [   ]

	Activity	Reason
☐		
☐		
☐		

	Step	Obstacle	Negative Feeling
☐			
☐			
☐			

A _____ who feels _____
    USER ROLE   NEGATIVE FEELING

about _____ needs to _____
       REASON   STEP

but faces _____
          OBSTACLE

UX Problem Statement Worksheet

Project name _____   Date: _____

User role: [   ]

	Activity	Reason
☐		
☐		
☐		

	Step	Obstacle	Negative Feeling
☐			
☐			
☐			

A _____ who feels _____
       USER ROLE   NEGATIVE FEELING

about _____ needs to _____
       REASON   STEP

but faces _____
       OBSTACLE

UX Problem Statement Worksheet

Project name _____   Date: _____

User role: [   ]

	Activity	Reason
☐		
☐		
☐		

	Step	Obstacle	Negative Feeling
☐			
☐			
☐			

A _____ who feels _____

       USER ROLE   NEGATIVE FEELING

about _____ needs to _____

       REASON   STEP

but faces _____

                 OBSTACLE

UX Problem Statement Worksheet

Project name _____   Date: _____

User role: [   ]

	Activity	Reason
☐		
☐		
☐		

	Step	Obstacle	Negative Feeling
☐			
☐			
☐			

A _____ who feels _____
   USER ROLE   NEGATIVE FEELING

about _____ needs to _____
         REASON   STEP

but faces _____
                OBSTACLE

UX Problem Statement Worksheet

Project name _____   Date: _____

User role: [   ]

	Activity	Reason
☐		
☐		
☐		

	Step	Obstacle	Negative Feeling
☐			
☐			
☐			

A _____ who feels _____

USER ROLE   NEGATIVE FEELING

about _____ needs to _____

REASON   STEP

but faces _____

OBSTACLE

UX Problem Statement Worksheet

Project name _____   Date: _____

User role: [   ]

	Activity	Reason
☐		
☐		
☐		

	Step	Obstacle	Negative Feeling
☐			
☐			
☐			

A _____ who feels _____
    USER ROLE   NEGATIVE FEELING

about _____ needs to _____
    REASON   STEP

but faces _____
                OBSTACLE

UX Problem Statement Worksheet

Project name _____   Date: _____

User role: _____

	Activity	Reason
☐		
☐		
☐		

	Step	Obstacle	Negative Feeling
☐			
☐			
☐			

A _____ who feels _____
   USER ROLE   NEGATIVE FEELING

about _____ needs to _____
      REASON   STEP

but faces _____
          OBSTACLE

UX Problem Statement Worksheet

Project name _____   Date: _____

User role: [   ]

	Activity	Reason
☐		
☐		
☐		

	Step	Obstacle	Negative Feeling
☐			
☐			
☐			

A _____ who feels _____
　　　　USER ROLE　　　　　　　　　　　　　　NEGATIVE FEELING

about _____ needs to _____
　　　　REASON　　　　　　　　　　　　　　　　STEP

but faces _____
　　　　　　　OBSTACLE

UX Problem Statement Worksheet

Project name _____   Date: _____

User role: [_____]

	Activity	Reason
☐		
☐		
☐		

	Step	Obstacle	Negative Feeling
☐			
☐			
☐			

A _____ who feels _____
      USER ROLE   NEGATIVE FEELING

about _____ needs to _____
        REASON   STEP

but faces _____
              OBSTACLE

UX Problem Statement Worksheet

Project name _____   Date: _____

User role: [   ]

	Activity	Reason
☐		
☐		
☐		

	Step	Obstacle	Negative Feeling
☐			
☐			
☐			

A _____ who feels _____
    USER ROLE   NEGATIVE FEELING

about _____ needs to _____
          REASON   STEP

but faces _____
              OBSTACLE

UX Problem Statement Worksheet

Project name _____   Date: _____

User role: [   ]

	Activity	Reason
☐		
☐		
☐		

	Step	Obstacle	Negative Feeling
☐			
☐			
☐			

A _____ who feels _____

USER ROLE   NEGATIVE FEELING

about _____ needs to _____

REASON   STEP

but faces _____

OBSTACLE

UX Problem Statement Worksheet

Project name _____   Date: _____

User role: [   ]

	Activity	Reason
☐		
☐		
☐		

	Step	Obstacle	Negative Feeling
☐			
☐			
☐			

A _____ who feels _____

       USER ROLE   NEGATIVE FEELING

about _____ needs to _____

       REASON   STEP

but faces _____

       OBSTACLE

UX Problem Statement Worksheet

Project name _____ Date: _____

User role: [   ]

	Activity	Reason
☐		
☐		
☐		

	Step	Obstacle	Negative Feeling
☐			
☐			
☐			

A _____ who feels _____
USER ROLE   NEGATIVE FEELING

about _____ needs to _____
REASON   STEP

but faces _____
OBSTACLE

UX Problem Statement Worksheet

Project name _____   Date: _____

User role: [   ]

	Activity	Reason
☐		
☐		
☐		

	Step	Obstacle	Negative Feeling
☐			
☐			
☐			

A _____ who feels _____
USER ROLE   NEGATIVE FEELING

about _____ needs to _____
REASON   STEP

but faces _____
OBSTACLE

UX Problem Statement Worksheet

Project name _____   Date:_____

User role: [_____]

	Activity	Reason
☐		
☐		
☐		

	Step	Obstacle	Negative Feeling
☐			
☐			
☐			

A _____ who feels _____
      USER ROLE   NEGATIVE FEELING

about _____ needs to _____
      REASON   STEP

but faces _____
                          OBSTACLE

UX Problem Statement Worksheet

Project name _____   Date: _____

User role: [   ]

	Activity	Reason
☐		
☐		
☐		

	Step	Obstacle	Negative Feeling
☐			
☐			
☐			

A _____ who feels _____
USER ROLE   NEGATIVE FEELING

about _____ needs to _____
REASON   STEP

but faces _____
OBSTACLE

UX Problem Statement Worksheet

Project name _____   Date: _____

User role: [   ]

	Activity	Reason
☐		
☐		
☐		

	Step	Obstacle	Negative Feeling
☐			
☐			
☐			

A _____ who feels _____

        USER ROLE   NEGATIVE FEELING

about _____ needs to _____

        REASON   STEP

but faces _____

                         OBSTACLE

UX Problem Statement Worksheet

Project name _____   Date: _____

User role: [   ]

	Activity	Reason
☐		
☐		
☐		

	Step	Obstacle	Negative Feeling
☐			
☐			
☐			

A _____ who feels _____
     USER ROLE   NEGATIVE FEELING

about _____ needs to _____
     REASON   STEP

but faces _____
     OBSTACLE

UX Problem Statement Worksheet

Project name _____   Date:_____

User role: [   ]

	Activity	Reason
☐		
☐		
☐		

	Step	Obstacle	Negative Feeling
☐			
☐			
☐			

A _____ who feels _____
     USER ROLE   NEGATIVE FEELING

about _____ needs to _____
            REASON   STEP

but faces _____
                    OBSTACLE

UX Problem Statement Worksheet

Project name _____   Date: _____

User role: [   ]

	Activity	Reason
☐		
☐		
☐		

	Step	Obstacle	Negative Feeling
☐			
☐			
☐			

A _____ who feels _____
       USER ROLE   NEGATIVE FEELING

about _____ needs to _____
       REASON   STEP

but faces _____
                 OBSTACLE

UX Problem Statement Worksheet

Project name _____   Date: _____

User role: [   ]

	Activity		Reason
☐			
☐			
☐			

	Step	Obstacle	Negative Feeling
☐			
☐			
☐			

A _____   who feels _____
  USER ROLE   NEGATIVE FEELING

about _____   needs to _____
  REASON   STEP

but faces _____
  OBSTACLE

UX Problem Statement Worksheet

Project name _____   Date: _____

User role: [   ]

	Activity	Reason
☐		
☐		
☐		

	Step	Obstacle	Negative Feeling
☐			
☐			
☐			

A _____ who feels _____
            USER ROLE   NEGATIVE FEELING

about _____ needs to _____
                REASON   STEP

but faces _____
                        OBSTACLE

UX Problem Statement Worksheet

Project name _____   Date: _____

User role: [   ]

	Activity	Reason
☐		
☐		
☐		

	Step	Obstacle	Negative Feeling
☐			
☐			
☐			

A _____ who feels _____
   USER ROLE   NEGATIVE FEELING

about _____ needs to _____
        REASON   STEP

but faces _____
           OBSTACLE

UX Problem Statement Worksheet

Project name _____   Date: _____

User role: [   ]

	Activity	Reason
☐		
☐		
☐		

	Step	Obstacle	Negative Feeling
☐			
☐			
☐			

A _____ who feels _____

　　　USER ROLE　　　　　　　　　　　　NEGATIVE FEELING

about _____ needs to _____

　　　REASON　　　　　　　　　　　　　　STEP

but faces _____

　　　　　　OBSTACLE

UX Problem Statement Worksheet

Project name _____   Date: _____

User role: [   ]

	Activity	Reason
☐		
☐		
☐		

	Step	Obstacle	Negative Feeling
☐			
☐			
☐			

A _____ who feels _____
   USER ROLE   NEGATIVE FEELING

about _____ needs to _____
       REASON   STEP

but faces _____
            OBSTACLE

UX Problem Statement Worksheet

Project name _____   Date: _____

User role: [   ]

	Activity	Reason
☐		
☐		
☐		

	Step	Obstacle	Negative Feeling
☐			
☐			
☐			

A _____ who feels _____

    USER ROLE   NEGATIVE FEELING

about _____ needs to _____

    REASON   STEP

but faces _____

    OBSTACLE

UX Problem Statement Worksheet

Project name _____   Date:_____

User role: [   ]

	Activity	Reason
☐		
☐		
☐		

	Step	Obstacle	Negative Feeling
☐			
☐			
☐			

A _____ who feels _____
          USER ROLE   NEGATIVE FEELING

about _____ needs to _____
          REASON   STEP

but faces _____
                OBSTACLE

UX Problem Statement Worksheet

Project name _____   Date: _____

User role: [   ]

	Activity	Reason
☐		
☐		
☐		

	Step	Obstacle	Negative Feeling
☐			
☐			
☐			

A _____ who feels _____
  USER ROLE   NEGATIVE FEELING

about _____ needs to _____
  REASON   STEP

but faces _____
  OBSTACLE

UX Problem Statement Worksheet

Project name _____   Date: _____

User role: [   ]

	Activity	Reason
☐		
☐		
☐		

	Step	Obstacle	Negative Feeling
☐			
☐			
☐			

A _____ who feels _____
         USER ROLE   NEGATIVE FEELING

about _____ needs to _____
          REASON   STEP

but faces _____
              OBSTACLE

UX Problem Statement Worksheet

Project name _____   Date: _____

User role: [_____]

	Activity	Reason
☐		
☐		
☐		

	Step	Obstacle	Negative Feeling
☐			
☐			
☐			

A _____ who feels _____
         USER ROLE   NEGATIVE FEELING

about _____ needs to _____
         REASON   STEP

but faces _____
              OBSTACLE

UX Problem Statement Worksheet

Project name _____   Date:_____

User role: [_____]

	Activity	Reason
☐		
☐		
☐		

	Step	Obstacle	Negative Feeling
☐			
☐			
☐			

A _____ who feels _____

          USER ROLE   NEGATIVE FEELING

about _____ needs to _____

          REASON   STEP

but faces _____

                   OBSTACLE

UX Problem Statement Worksheet

Project name _____   Date: _____

User role: [_____]

	Activity	Reason
☐		
☐		
☐		

	Step	Obstacle	Negative Feeling
☐			
☐			
☐			

A _____ who feels _____
   USER ROLE   NEGATIVE FEELING

about _____ needs to _____
      REASON   STEP

but faces _____
          OBSTACLE

UX Problem Statement Worksheet

Project name _____   Date:_____

User role: [   ]

	Activity	Reason
☐		
☐		
☐		

	Step	Obstacle	Negative Feeling
☐			
☐			
☐			

A _____ who feels _____

     USER ROLE   NEGATIVE FEELING

about _____ needs to _____

     REASON   STEP

but faces _____

               OBSTACLE

UX Problem Statement Worksheet

User role: [   ]

	Activity	Reason
☐		
☐		
☐		

	Step	Obstacle	Negative Feeling
☐			
☐			
☐			

A _____ who feels _____
    USER ROLE   NEGATIVE FEELING

about _____ needs to _____
       REASON   STEP

but faces _____
          OBSTACLE

UX Problem Statement Worksheet

Project name _____   Date:_____

User role: [   ]

	Activity	Reason
☐		
☐		
☐		

	Step	Obstacle	Negative Feeling
☐			
☐			
☐			

A _____ who feels _____
      USER ROLE   NEGATIVE FEELING

about _____ needs to _____
         REASON   STEP

but faces _____
              OBSTACLE

Takeaway notes:

_____

_____

_____

_____

_____

Year of use:

_____

www.ingramcontent.com/pod-product-compliance
Lightning Source LLC
Chambersburg PA
CBHW052036280526
45791CB00010B/2977